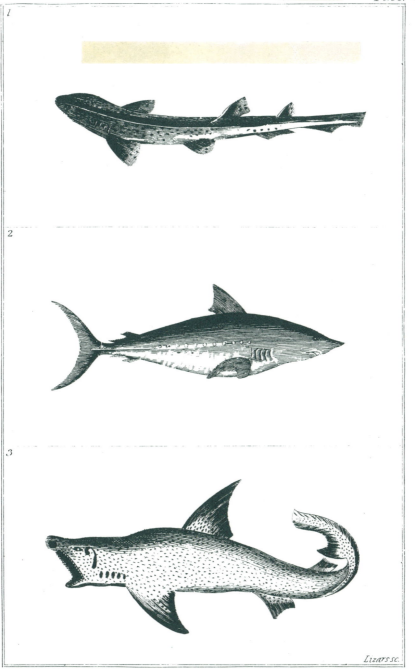

1. Lesser Spotted Shark 2. Porbeagle Dᵒ 3. White Dᵒ

Lizars sc.

FISH TALES

FISH TALES

STORIES FROM THE SEA

EDITED BY JOHN MILLER

DRAWINGS BY WILLIAM HOME LIZARS

STACKPOLE BOOKS

Copyright ©1993 by John Miller

Published by STACKPOLE BOOKS
Cameron and Kelker Streets
PO Box 1831
Harrisburg PA 17105

Printed in Hong Kong
Design by Big Fish Books, San Francisco

First Edition

10 9 8 7 6 5 4 3 2 1

Library of Congress Cataloging-in-Publication Data
Miller, John, 1959—
Fish tales : stories from the sea / edited by John Miller ;
drawings by William Home Lizars.
    p. cm.
Contents: Shining fish/Italo Calvino — The fish/Elizabeth
Bishop — Noa Noa/Paul Gauguin — The big fish/Blake Leland —
Dante and the lobster/Samuel Beckett — Man and the catfish/Zora
Neale Hurston — The baite/John Donne — The red mullet/Robert Penn
Warren — Squid/Herman Melville — The metamorphosis/Nick Lyons —
The great sea serpent/Hans Christian Andersen — Rain/Eduardo Galeano.
    ISBN 08117-0619-2: $30.00
1. Fishing—Literary collections. 2. Fishing stories.
3. Fishing—Pictorial works. I. Miller, John, 1959-
II. Lizars, W.J. (William Home), 1788-1859
PN6071.F47F57 1993
808.8'032162—dc20
                                        93-2665
                                        CIP

To my Pesce

PLATE 7.

PIMELODUS NOTATUS.

Lizars sc.

FISH TALES

J. Stewart delt.

TI

PLATE 29.

Lizars, sc.

A

PLATE 26.

Cychla monoculus.

INTRODUCTION

Trawling

EDINBURGH, SCOTLAND

IN THE NEW Haven market, you can choose from a variety of fish.

Each day, the fishmongers are out at dawn, steam-hosing sidewalks, scrubbing the wooden stalls, wheelbarrowing in loads of white ice and green fins.

As the Firth of Forth turns orange, their barking begins: "Herring!" "Monkfish!" "Flounder!" At the entrance to the market, we see two women hunching over creaking, wooden tubs labeled "INKFISH," deftly working the squid in a soup so purple it looks black.

It is now that earlybird shoppers begin their search for

the flattest flounder and the plumpest perch. Old Scottish men in sportcoats gingerly finger whelks and cockles. Working housewives test flying fish: "Too soft! Where are today's?!"

Huge cleavers muscle through the backs of fresh swordfish; in a dark corner a hydrahead of eels swirls in a brown stew. (Don't get too close; a live eel's blood is poisonous!)

The grandest display belongs to the northern herring: silver-green, ready to be hot-smoked, cold-smoked, pickled, or that most favored of delicacies—rolled in oatmeal and fried. Over there are blue mussels, with beards so tough ancient Greek fishermen wove gloves from them.

Directly ahead lie the villainous-looking scabbard fish, alongside plump, coinlike pompano. Both are surrounded by tiny smelts—a queer fish that smells of cucumber when fresh. Careful of your step, now: at the end of this row are the pesky, siren-red crayfish, notorious for crawling out of their tubs and across the floors. Look around and see more: cartilaginous, "bone-free" fishes (sharks, dogfish, rays); flatfish compressed vertically (skates and rays, with their white eyes and dark dorsal

PLATE 27

1. *The Fox Shark.* 2. *The Picked Dog Fish.*

Stewart delt

SERRAS

Native of the

PLATE 17.

Lizars sc.

UNCTATUS.

quibo, Guiana.

on top); flatfish compressed laterally (with both eyes migrated to the right side of their head, like flounder and sole; or to the left side, like turbot and brill). Fish after fish after fish!

This is what inspired William Home Lizars.

DANIEL LIZARS WAS the most famous engraver in all Edinburgh. His boy, William, like any good son, rebelled against dad's business and embarked on a painting career.

When William was only twenty-four, Daniel Lizars suddenly died. Despite some success in painting, the son decided to take over the family engraving business. William Lizars was an immediate hit, producing critically acclaimed illustrations of animals and humans, and, in the process, perfecting technical methods for book etching.

Two of his most notable works were the engravings for Sir William Jardine's behemoth, forty-two-volume *The Naturalist's Library* and a series of oversized plates for the never-published *Audubon's American Birds*.

In the 1840s, Lizars set out on his most ambitious project yet:

PLATE 8

1. Sea Loche, 2. Five Bearded Rockling.

to depict all of the creatures in the sea. But why? Sure, it was the age of enlightenment and scientists and illustrators were rushing to catalog everything in the world, but why spend so much time on just *fish*?

You could argue that fish are pretty important. After all, God flooded the entire world, destroying everything except the ark and the fish of the sea. (Why were they spared?) And man has been dependent on fish for his survival since 8,000 B.C. when the Egyptians invented the net and began exporting dried haddock. Then there's the fact that fish have possessed something mysteriously spiritual ever since Jesus talked them up in parable and miracle. (Remember his followers were to be "fishers of men." This religious symbolism reached frenzied proportions when persecuted Christians began using the fish as a secret symbol, as the Greek word for fish, ICHTHUS, formed an acrostic for the words Jesus, Christ, Son of God, Savior.)

And let's not forget the herring wars, Jonah and the whale, and the fact that many colonists came to America not to escape religious persecution but for the legendary cod fishing in Massachusetts (hence Cape Cod). There's no doubting that fish have played a key role in history, and it is true that an aspiring artist might want to catalog these slippery creatures. But look at these engravings. Something else is going on. These aren't just scientific plates— Lizars *liked* these fish. Maybe he remembered going with his dad to the New Haven market, wandering the aisles in awe. . . yes, even the little Lizars understood the intrigue, the mystery of *fish*.

HE IS NOT ALONE. For centuries, sleek fins have traversed dark, cold channels, flowing into the ink-blood of writers. And strange stories have come of it: Herman Melville sees his life pass before him as he witnesses a monstrous squid; Paul Gauguin catches a strange talisman in Tahitian waters; Elizabeth Bishop finds a surprise in a tremendous fish eye; Samuel Beckett plunges a live lobster into boiling water. . . and regrets it.

Fish Tales is no standard fishing anthology—here fish, not humans, take center stage. Each of these twelve stories, disparate as they are, has a deep, cool respect for the ocean and its finned inhabitants. The writers are trawling for information, for answers to shadowy questions that lie deep in the sea, our past home.

And they are looking to fish for clues. — J M

PLATE 10.

ARGUS PTERACLIS.

Lizars sc.

ITALO CALVINO

Shining Fish

THERE WAS A good old man whose sons had died, and he had no idea how he and his wife would now survive, for she too was old and ailing. Every day he went to the woods to gather firewood, and he would sell the bundle to buy bread and thus keep body and soul together.

One day as he was making his way through the woods and groaning, he met a gentleman with a long beard, who said, "I'm aware of all your troubles, and I will help you. Here is a purse containing a hundred ducats."

The old man took the purse and fainted. When he came to, the gentleman had disappeared. The old man went home and hid the hundred ducats under a heap of manure, without breathing a word to his wife. "If I gave her the money, it would be gone in no time . . . " Next day he returned to the woods, as usual.

That evening he found the table spread with a feast. "How did you manage to buy all this?" he asked, already alarmed.

"I sold the manure," said the wife.

"Wretch! Hidden in it were one hundred ducats!"

The next day the old man went through the woods sighing louder than ever. Again he met the gentleman with the long beard. "I am aware of your bad luck," said the gentleman. "Calm down. Here are one hundred ducats more."

This time the old man hid them in an ash pile. The next day his wife sold the ashes and fixed another hearty meal. When the old man came in and saw it, he couldn't eat a single bite and went off to bed tearing out his hair.

He was weeping in the woods the next morning, when back came the gentleman. "This time I shall give you no money. Take these twenty-four frogs out and sell them and with the proceeds buy yourself a fish—the biggest one to be had."

PLATE 15

1. Silvery Hair tail. 2. Scabbard Fish.

CIRRATED SAW-FISH.

PLATE 28.

Lizars sc.

The old man sold the frogs and bought a fish. At night he realized that it gleamed; it put out an intense light that shone all around. Holding it was like carrying a lantern. In the evening he hung it outside his window to keep it fresh. It was a dark and stormy night. The fishermen out at sea couldn't find their way in over the waves. Seeing the light at the window, they rowed toward it and were saved. They gave the old man half their haul and made an agreement with him that if he hung up the fish at the window every night, they would always divide their night's catch with him. That they did, and the good old man knew no more hardship.

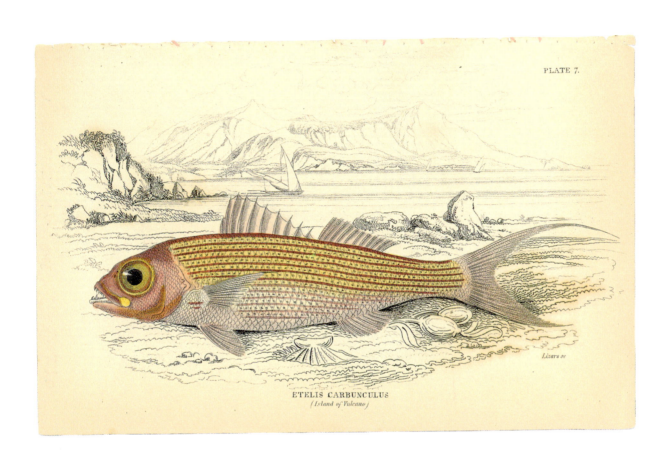

PLATE 7.

ETELIS CARBUNCULUS
(Island of Vulcano)

Lizars sc

ELIZABETH BISHOP

The Fish

I CAUGHT A tremendous fish
and held him beside the boat
half out of water, with my hook
fast in a corner of his mouth.
He didn't fight.
He hadn't fought at all.
He hung a grunting weight,
battered and venerable
and homely. Here and there
his brown skin hung in strips

PLATE 12.

OSTEOGLOSSUM AROWANA.

like ancient wallpaper,

and its pattern of darker brown was like wallpaper:

shapes like full-blown roses

stained and lost through age.

He was speckled with barnacles,

fine rosettes of lime,

and infested

with tiny white sea-lice,

and underneath two or three

rags of green weed hung down.

While his gills were breathing in

the terrible oxygen

—the frightening gills,

fresh and crisp with blood,

that can cut so badly—

I thought of the coarse white flesh

packed in like feathers,

the big bones and the little bones,

the dramatic reds and blacks

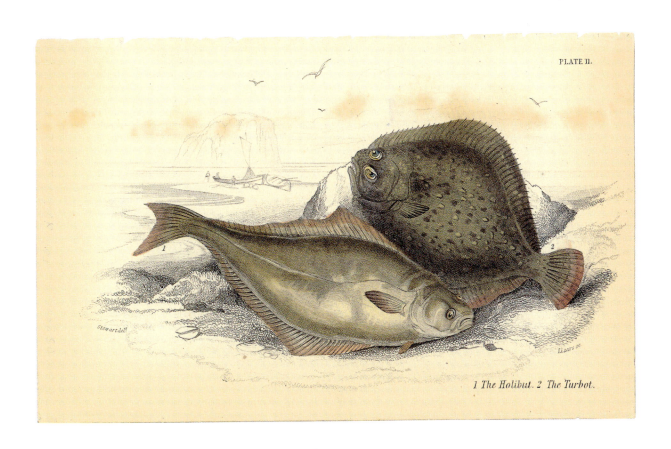

PLATE II.

1 The Holibut. 2 The Turbot.

PLATE 6

Cychla flavo-maculata

of his shiny entrails,

and the pink swim-bladder

like a big peony.

I looked into his eyes

which were far larger than mine

but shallower, and yellowed,

the irises backed and packed

with tarnished tinfoil

seen through the lenses

of old scratched isinglass.

They shifted a little, but not

to return my stare.

—It was more like the tipping

of an object toward the light.

I admired his sullen face,

the mechanism of his jaw,

and then I saw

that from his lower lip

—if you could call it a lip—

grim, wet, and weaponlike,

hung five old pieces of fish-line,

or four and a wire leader

with the swivel still attached,

with all their five big hooks

grown firmly in his mouth.

A green line, frayed at the end

where he broke it, two heavier lines,

and a fine black thread

still crimped from the strain and snap

when it broke and he got away.

Like medals with their ribbons

frayed and wavering,

a five-haired beard of wisdom

trailing from his aching jaw.

I stared and stared and victory filled up

the little rented boat,

from the pool of the bilge

where oil had spread a rainbow

around the rusted engine

to the bailer rusted orange,

the sun-cracked thwarts,

the oarlocks on their strings,

the gunnels—until everything

was rainbow, rainbow, rainbow!

And I let the fish go.

PLATE 4.

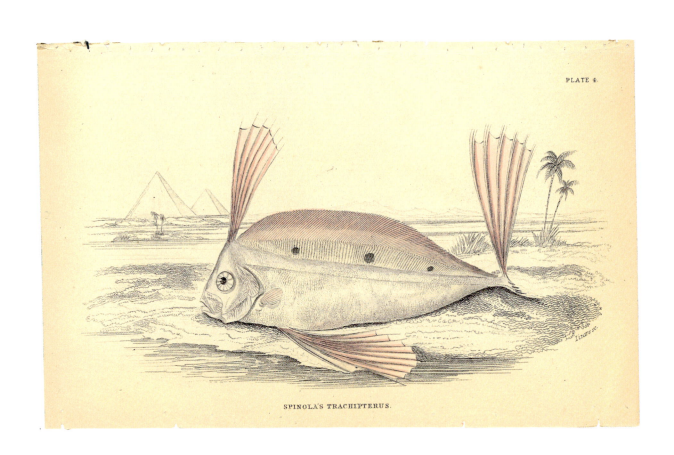

SPINOLA'S TRACHIPTERUS.

PAUL GAUGUIN

Noa Noa

SINCE ABOUT A fortnight there have been swarms of flies which are rare at other times, and they have become insupportable.

But the Maoris rejoice. The bonitoes and tunny-fish are coming to the surface. The flies proclaim that the season for fishing is at hand, the season of labor. But let us not forget that on Tahiti work itself is pleasure.

Every one was testing the strength of his lines and hooks. Women and children with unusual activity busied themselves in dragging nets, or rather long grates of cocoanut leaves, upon the seashore, and the corals which occupied the sea bottom between the land and the reefs. By this method certain small bait-fish of which the tunny-fish are very fond are caught.

Stewart del.

The Bas

PLATE 26.

Shark

Lizars sc.

After the preparations have been completed, which takes not less than three weeks, two large pirogues are tied together and launched upon the sea. They are furnished at the prow with a very long rod, which can be quickly raised by means of two lines fixed behind. The rod is supplied with a hook and bait. As soon as a fish has bitten it is drawn from the water and stored in the boat.

We set out upon the sea on a beautiful morning—naturally I participated in the festival—and soon were beyond the line of reefs. We ventured quite a distance out into the open sea. I still see a turtle with the head above water, watching us pass.

The fishermen were in a joyful mood, and rowed lustily.

We came to a spot which they called "tunny-hole" where the sea is very deep, opposite the grottoes of *Mara*.

There, it is said, the tunny-fish sleep during the night at a depth inaccessible to the sharks.

A cloud of sea-birds hovered above the hole on the alert for tunnies. When one of the fish appeared the birds dashed down with unbelievable rapidity, and then rose again with a ribbon of flesh in the beak.

Thus everywhere in the sea and in the air, and even in our

pirogues carnage is contemplated or carried out.

When I ask my companions why they do not let a long line down to the bottom of the "tunny-hole," they reply to me that it is impossible since it is a sacred place.

"The god of the sea dwells there."

I suspect that there is a legend behind this, and without difficulty I succeed in getting them to tell it to me.

ROÜA HATOU, a kind of Tahitian Neptune, slept here at the bottom of the sea.

A Maori was once foolhardy enough to fish here, and his hook caught in the hair of the god, and the god awoke.

Filled with wrath he rose to the surface to see who had the temerity to disturb his sleep. When he saw that the guilty one was a man, he decided that all the human race must perish to expiate the impiety of one.

By some mysterious indulgence, however, the author himself of the crime escaped punishment.

The god ordered him to go with all his family upon *Toa Marama*, which according to some is an island or mountain, and

PLATE 6

Stewart del.

Lizars sc.

Fifteen Spined Stickleback nest and eggs.

according to others a pirogue or an "ark."

When the fisher and his family had gone to the designated place, the waters of the ocean began to rise. Slowly they covered even the highest mountains, and all the living perished except those who had taken flight upon (or in) *Toa Marama*.

Later they repeopled the islands.

WE LEFT THE "tunny-hole" behind us, and the master of the pirogue designated a man to extend the rod over the sea and cast out the hook.

We waited long minutes, but not a bite came.

It was now the turn of another oarsman; this time a magnificent tunny-fish bit and made the rod bend downward. Four powerful arms raised it by pulling at the ropes behind, and the tunny appeared on the surface. But simultaneously a huge shark leaped across the waves. He struck a few times with his terrible teeth, and nothing was left on the hook except the head.

The master gave a signal. I cast out the hook.

In a very short time we caught an enormous tunny. Without paying much attention to it, I heard my companions laughing and

ACANTHICUS HISTRIX.
Fort St Joaquim in the distance.

PLATE 1.

Lizars sc.

whispering among themselves. Killed by blows on the head the animal quivered in its death agony in the bottom of the boat. Its body was transformed into a gleaming many-faceted mirror, sending out the lights of a thousand fires.

The second time I was lucky again.

Decidedly, the Frenchman brought good luck. My companions joyously congratulated me, insisted that I was a lucky fellow, and I, quite proud of myself, did not make denial.

But amid all this unanimity of praise, I distinguished, as at the time of my first exploit, an unexplained whispering and laughter.

The fishing continued until evening.

When the store of small bait-fish was exhausted, the sun lighted red flames on the horizon, and our pirogue was laden with ten magnificent tunny-fish.

They were preparing to return.

While things were being put in order, I asked one of the young fellows as to the meaning of the exchange of whispered words and the laughter which had accompanied my two captures. He refused to reply. But I was insistent, knowing very well how little power of resistance a Maori has and how quickly he gives in to energetic pressure.

Finally he confided to me. If the fish is caught with the hook in the lower jaw—and both my tunnies were thus caught—it signifies that the *vahina* is unfaithful during the *tané's* absence.

I smiled incredulously.

And we returned.

Night falls quickly in the tropics. It is important to forestall it. Twenty-two alert oars dipped and re-dipped simultaneously into the sea, and to stimulate themselves the rowers uttered cries in rhythm with their strokes. Our pirogues left a phosphorescent wake behind.

I had the sensation of a mad flight. The angry masters of the ocean were pursuing us. Around us the frightened and curious fish leaped like fantastic troupes of indefinite figures.

In two hours we were approaching the outermost reefs.

The sea beats furiously here, and the passage is dangerous on account of the surf. It is not an easy maneuver to steer the pirogue correctly. But the natives are skillful. Much interested and not entirely without fear I followed the operation which was executed perfectly.

The land ahead of us was illumined with moving fires.

They were enormous torches made of the dry branches of the cocoanut-trees. It was a magnificent picture. The families of the fishermen were awaiting us on the sand on the edge of the illumined water. Some of the figures remained seated and motionless; others ran along the shore waving the torches; the children leaped hither and thither and their shrill cries could be heard from afar.

With powerful movement the pirogue ran up on the sand.

Immediately they proceeded to the division of the booty.

All the fish were laid on the ground, and the master divided them into as many equal parts as there were persons—men, women, and children—who had taken part in the fishing for the tunnies or in the catching of the little fish used for bait.

There were thirty-seven parts.

Without loss of time, my *vahina* took the hatchet, split some wood, and lighted the fire while I was changing clothes and putting on some wraps on account of the evening chill.

One of our two parts was cooked; her own Tehura put away raw.

Then she asked me fully about the various happenings of the day, and I willingly satisfied her curiosity. With child-like contentment she took pleasure in everything, and I watched her

PLATE 16

1 Hawkins Gymnetrus. 2 Red Band Fish.

PLATE 23

Black Mouthed Dog Fish

without letting her suspect the secret thoughts which were occupying me. Deep down within me without any plausible cause, a feeling of disquietude had awakened which it was no longer possible to calm. I was burning to put a certain question to Tehura, a certain question … and it was vain for me to ask of myself, "To what good?" I, myself, replied, "Who knows?"

THE HOUR OF going to bed had come, and, when we were both stretched out side by side, I suddenly asked,

"Have you been sensible?"

"Yes."

"And your lover to-day, was he to your liking?"

"I have no lover."

"You lie. The fish has spoken."

Tehura raised herself and looked fixedly at me. Her face had imprinted upon it an extraordinary expression of mysticism and majesty and strange grandeur with which I was unfamiliar and which I would never have expected to see in her naturally joyous and still almost child-like face.

The atmosphere in our little hut was transformed. *I felt that something sublime had risen up between us.* In spite of myself I yielded to the influence of Faith, and I was waiting for a message from above. I did not doubt that this message would come; but the sterile vanity of our skepticism still had its influence over me, in spite of the glowing sureness of a faith like this rooted though it was in some superstition or other.

Tehura softly crept to our door to make sure that it was tightly shut, and having come back as far as the center of the room she spoke aloud this prayer:

> *Save me! Save me!*
> *It is evening, it is evening of the Gods!*
> *Watch close over me, Oh my God!*
> *Watch over me, Oh my Lord!*
> *Preserve me from enchantments and evil counsels.*
> *Preserve me from sudden death,*
> *And from those who send evil and curses;*
> *Guard me from quarrels over the division of the lands,*
> *That peace may reign about us!*
> *Oh my God, protect me from raging warriors!*
> *Protect me from him who in erring threatens me,*

Who takes pleasure in making me tremble,

Against him whose hairs are always bristling!

To the end that I and my soul may live,

Oh my God!

That evening, I verily joined in prayer with Tehura.

When she had finished her prayer, she came over to me and said with her eyes full of tears,

"You must strike me, strike me many, many times."

In the profound expression of this face and in the perfect beauty of this statue of living flesh, I had a vision of the divinity herself who had been conjured up by Tehura.

Let my hands be eternally cursed if they will raise themselves against a masterpiece of nature!

Thus naked, the eyes tranquil in the tears, she seemed to me robed in a mantle of orange-yellow purity, in the orange-yellow mantle of Bhixu.

She repeated,

"You must strike me, strike me many, many times; otherwise you will be angry for a long time and you will be sick."

I kissed her.

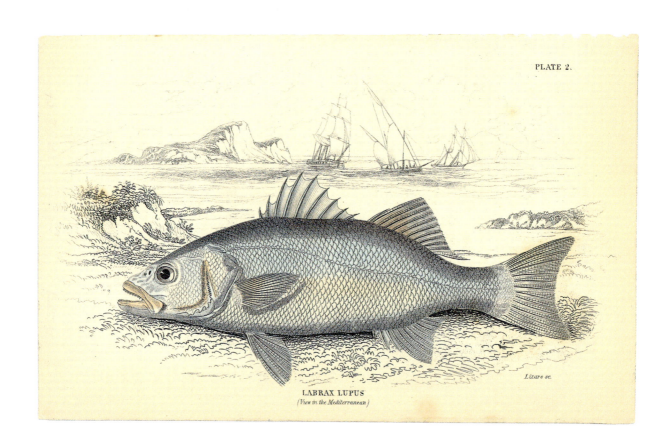

PLATE 2.

LABRAX LUPUS
(View in the Mediterranean)

Lizars sc.

And now that I love without suspicion and love her as much as I admire her, I murmur these words of Buddha to myself,

"By kindness you must conquer anger; by goodness evil; and by the truth lies."

That night was divine, more than any of the others—and the day rose radiant.

Early in the morning her mother brought us some fresh cocoanuts.

With a glance she questioned Tehura. She *knew*.

With a fine play of expression, she said to me,

"You went fishing yesterday. Did all go well?"

I replied,

"I hope soon to go again."

BLAKE LELAND

The Big Fish

SET TRUTH TO music and you get the sea
  Slowly at first, seeping under the door:
Whispering insistencies of foam,
  Soft sucking sounds, soak into the carpet
Which is blue, figured with flowers
  And Euclidean birds escaped from books.

After a while you move about the room
  Wet to the ankles, sloshing as you walk,
Distracted by the rhythmic beating at the door
  And the smell of salt, and the black muck silt

PLATE 29.

COMMON SWORD-FISH.

PLATE 22.

Trygon strogylopterus.

Stewart delt

Lizars sc.

FISH TALES

That glitters even as the lamp shorts out
    Revealing what might be moonlight—
A luminous, fluent refraction
    Wiggling through the watery windows.

Sea stars and horseshoe crabs with radiant
    Or bisected symmetries scuttle in
Across the carpet, under easy chairs; they knock
    Against the coffee table's sunken legs
And touch at your toes as if they might be
    Succulent and essential morsels.

The music is ancient and simple
    And terrifying: the embroidered birds
Of your canny, dry considerations
    Never sang like this, never managed such
Motile, saline chanteys, no.
    And now the fish pluck your buttons off,
The octopus walks away in your trousers,

And mussels make their beds amongst your shoes.

You say a deep-blue *Ave Mare* as you breathe
   Strange and easy while the current swells,
Lifts and pulls you, lifts your heart,
   Lifts and floats it so that you become
The buoyant core of your veracious room,
   The moist monster poised in its archaic dream.

Once you thought it best only to live
   At the sea's edge, to listen as kelp tongues
And tide-tumbled smoothed shards of porcelain
   Compared their histories, while you took notes;
And that sea-glass calculus seemed true enough.
   But who standing now where the shore keeps time
Will hear the merest rumor of your sunken house,
   Or, multiplying atmospheres, guess your deep
      appropriate form?

He will not know what way you move

    In the phosphorescent decorations of the dark:

He will not know how you dispose,

    By an arrangement of fins, his own profound

Dumb adumbration of the blood's first beat

    Beneath the singsong surface of the sea.

PLATE 31.

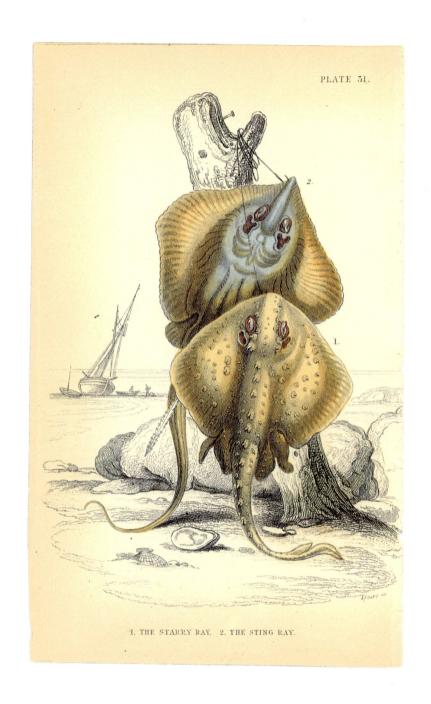

1. THE STARRY RAY.   2. THE STING RAY.

SAMUEL BECKETT

Dante and the Lobster

IT WAS MORNING and Belacqua was stuck in the first of the canti in the moon. He was so bogged that he could move neither backward nor forward. Blissful Beatrice was there, Dante also, and she explained the spots on the moon to him. She shewed him in the first place where he was at fault, then she put up her own explanation. She had it from God, therefore he could rely on its being accurate in every particular. All he had to do was to follow her step by step. Part one, the refutation, was plain sailing. She made her point clearly, she said what she had to say without fuss or loss of time. But part two, the demonstration, was so dense that Belacqua could not make head or tail of it. The disproof, the reproof, that was patent. But then came the proof, a rapid shorthand of the real facts, and Belacqua was bogged indeed. Bored also, impatient to get on to Piccarda. Still he pored over the enigma, he would not concede himself conquered, he would understand at least the meanings of the words, the order in which they were spoken and the nature of the satisfaction that they conferred on the misinformed poet, so that when they were ended he was refreshed and could raise his heavy head, intending to return thanks and make formal retraction of his old opinion.

He was still running his brain against this impenetrable passage when he heard midday strike. At once he switched his mind off its task. He scooped his fingers under the book and shovelled it back till it lay wholly on his palms. The Divine Comedy face upward on the lectern of his palms. Thus disposed he raised it under his nose and there he slammed it shut. He held it aloft for a time, squinting at it angrily, pressing the boards inwards with the heels of his hands. Then he laid it aside.

He leaned back in his chair to feel his mind subside and the itch of this mean quodlibet die down. Nothing could be done until his mind got better and was still, which gradually it did. Then he ventured to consider what he had to do next. There was always something that one had to do next. Three large obligations presented themselves. First lunch, then the lobster, then the Italian lesson. That would do to be going on with. After the Italian lesson he had no very clear idea. No doubt some niggling curriculum had been drawn up by someone for the late afternoon and evening, but he did not know what. In any case it did not matter. What did matter was: one, lunch; two, the lobster; three, the Italian lesson. That was more than enough to be going on with.

Lunch, to come off at all, was a very nice affair. If his lunch was to be enjoyable, and it could be very enjoyable indeed, he must be left in absolute tranquility to prepare it. But if he were disturbed now, if some brisk tattler were to come bouncing in now big with a big idea or a petition, he might just as well not eat at all, for the food would turn to bitterness on his palate, or, worse again, taste of nothing. He must be left strictly alone, he must have complete quiet and privacy to prepare the food for his lunch.

The first thing to do was to lock the door. Now nobody

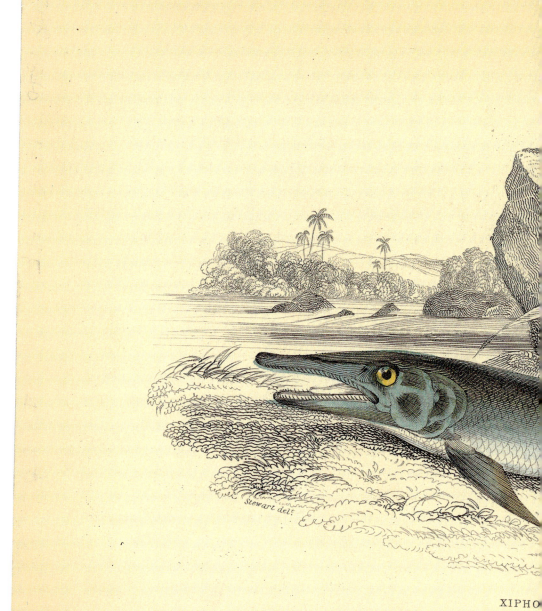

Stewart delt.

XIPHO

PLATE 23

Lizars sc.

OCELLATUM.

could come at him. He deployed an old *Herald* and smoothed it out
on the table. The rather handsome face of McCabe the assassin
stared up at him. Then he lit the gas-ring and unhooked the square
flat toaster, asbestos grill, from its nail and set it precisely on the
flame. He found he had to lower the flame. Toast must not on any
account be done too rapidly. For bread to be toasted as it ought,
through and through, it must be done on a mild steady flame.
Otherwise you only charred the outsides and left the pith as sodden
as before. If there was one thing he abominated more than another it
was to feel his teeth meet in a bathos of pith and dough. And it was
so easy to do the thing properly. So, he thought, having regulated
the flow and adjusted the grill, by the time I have the bread cut that
will be just right. Now the long barrel-loaf came out of its biscuit-tin
and had its end evened off on the face of McCabe. Two inexorable
drives with the bread-saw and a pair of neat rounds of raw bread, the
main elements of his meal, lay before him, awaiting his pleasure.
The stump of the loaf went back into prison, the crumbs, as though
there were no such thing as a sparrow in the wide world, were
swept in a fever away, and the slices snatched up and carried to the

PLATE 16.

PORCUPINE DIODON

PLATE 18.

BLAINVILLES PIKED DOG FISH.

grill. All these preliminaries were very hasty and impersonal.

It was now that real skill began to be required, it was at this point that the average person began to make a hash of the entire proceedings. He laid his cheek against the soft of the bread, it was spongy and warm, alive. But he would very soon take that plush feel off it, by God but he would very quickly take that fat white look off its face. He lowered the gas a suspicion and plaqued one flabby slab down on the glowing fabric, but very pat and precise, so that the whole resembled the Japanese flag. Then on top, there not being room for the two to do evenly side by side, and if you did not do them evenly you might just as well save yourself the trouble of doing them at all, the other round was set to warm. When the first candidate was done, which was only when it was black through and through, it changed places with its comrade, so that now it in its turn lay on top, done to a dead end, black and smoking, waiting till as much could be said of the other.

For the tiller of the field the thing was simple, he had it from his mother. The spots were Cain with his truss of thorns, dispossessed, cursed from the earth, fugitive and vagabond. The moon was that countenance fallen and branded, seared with the first stigma of God's pity, that an outcast might not die quickly. It was a mix-up in the mind of the tiller, but that did not matter. It had been good enough for his mother, it was good enough for him.

Belacqua on his knees before the flame, poring over the grill, controlled every phase of the broiling. It took time, but if a thing was worth doing at all it was worth doing well, that was a true saying. Long before the end the room was full of smoke and the reek of burning. He switched off the gas, when all that human care and skill could do had been done, and restored the toaster to its nail. This was an act of dilapidation, for it seared a great weal in the paper. This was hooliganism pure and simple. What the hell did he care? Was it his wall? The same hopeless paper had been there fifty years. It was livid with age. It could not be disimproved.

Next a thick paste of Savora, salt and Cayenne on each round, well worked in while the pores were still open with the heat. No butter, God forbid, just a good foment of mustard and salt and pepper on each round. Butter was a blunder, it made the toast soggy. Buttered toast was all right for Senior Fellows and Salvationists, for

such as had nothing but false teeth in their heads. It was no good at
all to a fairly strong young rose like Belacqua. This meal that he was
at such pains to make ready, he would devour it with a sense of
rapture and victory, it would be like smiting the sledded Polacks on
the ice. He would snap at it with closed eyes, he would gnash it into
a pulp, he would vanquish it utterly with his fangs. Then the
anguish of pungency, the pang of the spices, as each mouthful died,
scorching his palate, bringing tears.

But he was not yet all set, there was yet much to be done.
He had burnt his offering, he had not fully dressed it. Yes, he had
put the horse behind the tumbrel.

He clapped the toasted rounds together, he brought them
smartly together like cymbals, they clave the one to the other on the
viscid salve of Savora. Then he wrapped them up for the time being
in any old sheet of paper. Then he made himself ready for the road.

Now the great thing was to avoid being accosted. To be
stopped at this stage and have conversational nuisance committed
all over him would be a disaster. His whole being was straining
forward towards the joy in store. If he were accosted now he might

just as well fling his lunch into the gutter and walk straight back
home. Sometimes his hunger, more of mind, I need scarcely say, than
of body, for this meal amounted to such a frenzy that he would not
have hesitated to strike any man rash enough to buttonhole and
baulk him, he would have shouldered him out of his path without
ceremony. Woe betide the meddler who crossed him when his mind
was really set on this meal.

He threaded his way rapidly, his head bowed, through a
familiar labyrinth of lands and suddenly dived into a little family
grocery. In the shop they were not surprised. Most days, about this
hour, he shot in off the street in this way.

The slab of cheese was prepared. Separated since morning
from the piece, it was only waiting for Belacqua to call and take it.
Gorgonzola cheese. He knew a man who came from Gorgonzola, his
name was Angelo. He had been born in Nice but all his youth had
been spent in Gorgonzola. He knew where to look for it. Every day
it was there, in the same corner, waiting to be called for. They were
very decent obliging people.

He looked sceptically at the cut of cheese. He turned it over

Mailed Gurnard.

on its back to see was the other side any better. The other side was
worse. They had laid it better side up, they had practised that little
deception. Who shall blame them? He rubbed it. It was sweating.
That was something. He stooped and smelt it. A faint fragrance of
corruption. What good was that? He didn't want fragrance, he
wasn't a bloody gourmet, he wanted a good stench. What he wanted
was a good green stenching rotten lump of Gorgonzola cheese, alive,
and by God he would have it.

He looked fiercely at the grocer.

"What's that?" he demanded.

The grocer writhed.

"Well?" demanded Belacqua, he was without fear when
roused, "is that the best you can do?"

"In the length and breadth of Dublin" said the grocer "you
won't find a rottener bit this minute."

Belacqua was furious. The impudent dogsbody, for two pins
he would assault him.

"It won't do" he cried, "do you hear me, it won't do at all.
I won't have it." He ground his teeth.

The grocer, instead of simply washing his hands like Pilate, flung out his arms in a wild crucified gesture of supplication. Sullenly Belacqua undid his packet and slipped the cadaverous tablet of cheese between the hard cold black boards of the toast. He stumped to the door where he whirled round however.

"You heard me?" he cried.

"Sir" said the grocer. This was not a question, nor yet an expression of acquiescence. The tone in which it was let fall made it quite impossible to know what was in the man's mind. It was a most ingenious riposte.

"I tell you" said Belacqua with great heat "this won't do at all. If you can't do better than this" he raised the hand that held the packet "I shall be obliged to go for my cheese elsewhere. Do you mark me?"

"Sir" said the grocer.

He came to the threshold of his store and watched the indignant customer hobble away. Belacqua had a spavined gait, his feet were in ruins, he suffered with them almost continuously. Even in the night they took no rest, or next to none. For then the

Stewart del.

1 *The Sole.* 2 *The Variegated Sole*

PLATE 12.

1

Lizars sc.

cramps took over from the corns and hammer-toes, and carried on. So that he would press the fringes of his feet desperately against the end-rail of the bed or, better again, reach down with his hand and drag them up and back towards the instep. Skill and patience could disperse the pain, but there it was, complicating his night's rest.

The grocer, without closing his eyes or taking them off the receding figure, blew his nose in the skirt of his apron. Being a warm-hearted human man he felt sympathy and pity for this queer customer who always looked ill and dejected. But at the same time he was a small tradesman, don't forget that, with a small tradesman's sense of personal dignity and what was what. Thruppence, he cast it up, thruppence worth of cheese per day, one and a tanner per week. No, he would fawn on no man for that, no, not on the best in the land. He had his pride.

Stumbling along by devious ways towards the lowly public where he was expected, in the sense that the entry of his grotesque person would provoke no comment or laughter, Belacqua gradually got the upper hand of his choler. Now that lunch was as good as a *fait accompli*, because the incontinent bosthoons of his own class, itching to pass on a big idea or inflict an appointment, were seldom at large in this shabby quarter of the city, he was free to consider items two and three, the lobster and the lesson, in closer detail.

At a quarter to three he was due at the School. Say five to three. The public closed, the fish-monger reopened, at half-past two. Assuming then that his lousy old bitch of an aunt had given her order in good time that morning, with strict injunctions that it should be ready and waiting so that her blackguard boy should on no account be delayed when he called for it first thing in the afternoon, it would be time enough if he left the public as it closed, he could remain on till the last moment. Benissimo. He had half-a-crown. That was two pints of draught anyway and perhaps a bottle to wind up with. Their bottled stout was particularly excellent and well up. And he would still be left with enough coppers to buy a *Herald* and take a tram if he felt tired or was pinched for time. Always assuming, of course, that the lobster was all ready to be handed over. God damn these tradesmen, he thought, you can never rely on them. He had not done an exercise but that did not matter. His Professoressa was so charming and remarkable.

Signorina Adriana Ottolenghi! He did not believe it possible for a woman to be more intelligent or better informed than the little Ottolenghi. So he had set her on a pedestal in his mind, apart from other women. She had said last day that they would read *Il Cinque Maggio* together. But she would not mind if he told her, as he proposed to, in Italian, he would frame a shining phrase on his way from the public, that he would prefer to postpone the *Cinque Maggio* to another occasion. Manzoni was an old woman, Napoleon was another. *Napoleon di mezza calzetta, fa l'amore a Giacominetta.* Why did he think of Manzoni as an old woman? Why did he do him that injustice? Pellico was another. They were all old maids, suffragettes. He must ask his Signorina where he could have received that impression, that the 19th century in Italy was full of old hens trying to cluck like Pindar. Carducci was another. Also about the spots on the moon. If she could not tell him there and then she would make it up, only too gladly, against the next time. Everything was all set now and in order. Bating, of course, the lobster, which had to remain an incalculable factor. He must just hope for the best. And expect the worst, he thought gaily, diving into the public, as usual.

Belacqua drew near to the school, quite happy, for all had gone swimmingly. The lunch had been a notable success, it would abide as a standard in his mind. Indeed he could not imagine its ever being superseded. And such a pale soapy piece of cheese to prove so strong! He must only conclude that he had been abusing himself all these years in relating the strength of cheese directly to its greenness. We live and learn, that was a true saying. Also his teeth and jaws had been in heaven, splinters of vanquished toast spraying forth at each gnash. It was like eating glass. His mouth burned and ached with the exploit. Then the food had been further spiced by the intelligence, transmitted in a low tragic voice across the counter by Oliver the improver, that the Malahide murderer's petition for mercy, signed by half the land, having been rejected, the man must swing at dawn in Mountjoy and nothing could save him. Ellis the hangman was even now on his way. Belacqua, tearing at the sandwich and swilling the precious stout, pondered on McCabe in his cell.

The lobster was ready after all, the man handed it over instanter, and with such a pleasant smile. Really a little bit of courtesy and goodwill went a long way in this world. A smile and a

PLATE 14

1 The Unctuous Sucker. 2 The Common Remora.

Stewart del.t

Lizars sc.

cheerful word from a common working-man and the face of the world was brightened. And it was so easy, a mere question of muscular control.

"Lepping" he said cheerfully, handing it over.

"Lepping?" said Belacqua. What on earth was that?

"Lepping fresh, sir" said the man, "fresh in this morning."

Now Belacqua, on the analogy of mackerel and other fish that he had heard described as lepping fresh when they had been taken but an hour or two previously, supposed the man to mean that the lobster had very recently been killed.

Signorina Adriana Ottolenghi was waiting in the little front room off the hall, which Belacqua was naturally inclined to think of rather as the vestibule. That was her room, the Italian room. On the same side, but at the back, was the French room. God knows where the German room was. Who cared about the German room anyway?

He hung up his coat and hat, laid the long knobby brown-paper parcel on the hall-table, and went prestly in to the Ottolenghi.

After about half-an-hour of this and that obiter, she

complimented him on his grasp of the language.

"You make rapid progress" she said in her ruined voice.

There subsisted as much of the Ottolenghi as might be expected to of the person of a lady of a certain age who had found being young and beautiful and pure more of a bore than anything else.

Belacqua, dissembling his great pleasure, laid open the moon enigma.

"Yes" she said "I know the passage. It is a famous teaser. Off-hand I cannot tell you, but I will look it up when I get home."

The sweet creature! She would look it up in her big Dante when she got home. What a woman!

"It occurred to me" she said "apropos of I don't know what, that you might do worse than make up Dante's rare movements of compassion in Hell. That used to be" her past tenses were always sorrowful "a favourite question."

He assumed an expression of profundity.

"In that connexion" he said "I recall one superb pun anyway: '*qui vive la pieta quando è ben morta . . .* '"

She said nothing.

"Is it not a great phrase?" he gushed.

She said nothing.

"Now" he said like a fool "I wonder how you could translate that?"

Still she said nothing. Then:

"Do you think" she murmured "it is absolutely necessary to translate it?"

Sounds as of conflict were borne in from the hall. Then silence. A knuckle tambourined on the door, it flew open and lo it was Mlle Glain, the French instructress, clutching her cat, her eyes out on stalks, in a state of the greatest agitation.

"Oh" she gasped "forgive me. I intrude, but what was in the bag?"

"The bag?" said the Ottolenghi.

Mlle Glain took a French step forward.

"The parcel" she buried her face in the cat "the parcel in the hall."

Belacqua spoke up composedly.

"Mine" he said, "a fish."

He did not know the French for lobster. Fish would do very well. Fish had been good enough for Jesus Christ, Son of God, Saviour. It was good enough for Mlle Glain.

"Oh" said Mlle Glain, inexpressibly relieved, "I caught him in the nick of time." She administered a tap to the cat. "He would have tore it to flitters."

Belacqua began to feel a little anxious.

"Did he actually get at it?" he said.

"No no" said Mlle Glain "I caught him just in time. But I did not know" with a blue-stocking snigger "what it might be, so I thought I had better come and ask."

Base prying bitch.

The Ottolenghi was faintly amused.

"*Puisqu'il n'y a pas de mal . . .*" she said with great fatigue and elegance.

"*Heureusement*" it was clear at once that Mlle Glain was devout "*heureusement.*"

Chastening the cat with little skelps she took herself off.

PLATE 18.

Gymnotus electricus.

The grey hairs of her maidenhead screamed at Belacqua. A virginal blue-stocking, honing after a penny's worth of scandal.

"Where were we?" said Belacqua.

But Neopolitan patience has its limits.

"Where are we ever?" cried the Ottolenghi, "where we were, as we were."

BELACQUA DREW NEAR to the house of his aunt. Let us call it winter, that dusk may fall now and a moon rise. At the corner of the street a horse was down and a man sat on his head. I know, thought Belacqua, that that is considered the right thing to do. But why? A lamplighter flew by on his bike, tilting with his pole at the standards, jousting a little yellow light into the evening. A poorly dressed couple stood in the bay of a pretentious gateway, she sagging against the railings, her head lowered, he standing facing her. He stood up close to her, his hands dangled by his sides. Where we were, thought Belacqua, as we were. He walked on, gripping his parcel. Why not piety and pity both, even down below? Why not mercy and Godliness together? A little mercy in the stress of sacrifice, a little mercy to rejoice against judgment. He thought of Jonah and the gourd and the pity of a jealous God on Nineveh. And poor McCabe, he would get it in the neck at dawn. What was he doing now, how was he feeling? He would relish one more meal, one more night.

His aunt was in the garden, tending whatever flowers die at that time of year. She embraced him and together they went down into the bowels of the earth, into the kitchen in the basement. She took the parcel and undid it and abruptly the lobster was on the table, on the oilcloth, discovered.

"They assured me it was fresh" said Belacqua.

Suddenly he saw the creature move, this neuter creature. Definitely it changed its position. His hand flew to his mouth.

"Christ!" he said "it's alive."

His aunt looked at the lobster. It moved again. It made a faint nervous act of life on the oilcloth. They stood above it, looking down on it, exposed cruciform on the oilcloth. It shuddered again. Belacqua felt he would be sick.

"My God" he whined "it's alive, what'll we do?"

The aunt simply had to laugh. She bustled off to the pantry to fetch her smart apron, leaving him goggling down at the lobster, and came back with it on and her sleeves rolled up, all business.

"Well" she said "it is to be hoped so, indeed."

"All this time" muttered Belacqua. Then, suddenly aware of her hideous equipment: "What are you going to do?" he cried.

"Boil the beast" she said, "what else?"

"But it's not dead" protested Belacqua "you can't boil it like that."

She looked at him in astonishment. Had he taken leave of his senses?

"Have sense" she said sharply, "lobsters are always boiled alive. They must be." She caught up the lobster and laid it on its back. It trembled. "They feel nothing" she said.

In the depths of the sea it had crept into the cruel pot. For hours, in the midst of its enemies, it had breathed secretly. It had survived the Frenchwoman's cat and his witless clutch. Now it was going alive into scalding water. It had to. Take into the air my quiet breath.

Belacqua looked at the old parchment of her face, grey in the dim kitchen.

"You make a fuss" she said angrily "and upset me and then lash into it for your dinner."

SHE LIFTED THE lobster clear of the table. It had about thirty seconds to live.

Well, thought Belacqua, it's quick death, God help us all.

It is not.

PLATE 23.

DIACOPE RIVULATA

ZORA NEAL HURSTON

Man and the Cat-fish

NOW TAKE CAT-FISH for instances. Ah knows a man dat useter go fishin' every Sunday. His wife begged him not to do it and his pastor strained wid him for years but it didn't do no good. He just would go ketch him a fish every Sabbath. One Sunday he went and just as soon as he got to de water he seen a great big ole cat-fish up under some water lilies pickin' his teeth with his fins. So de man baited his pole and dropped de hook right down in front of de big fish. Dat cat grabbed de hook and took out for deep water. De man held on and pretty soon dat fish pulled him in. He couldn't git out. Some folks on de way to church seen him and run down to de water but he was in too deep. So he went down de first time

85

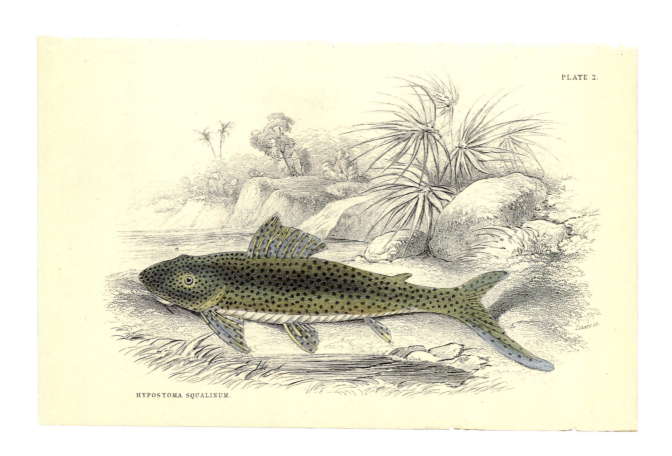

PLATE 2.

HYPOSTOMA SQUALINUM.

and when he come up he hollered—"Tell my wife." By dat time de fish pulled him under again. When he come up he hollered, "Tell my wife—" and went down again. When he come up de third time he said: "Tell my wife to fear God and cat-fish," and went down for de last time and he never come up no mo'.

JOHN DONNE

The Baite

COME LIVE WITH mee, and bee my love,
And wee will some new pleasures prove
Of golden sands, and christall brookes,
With silken lines, and silver hookes.

There will the river whispering runne
Warm'd by thy eyes, more than the Sunne.
And there th'inamor'd fish will stay,
Begging themselves they may betray.

When thou wilt swimme in that live bath,

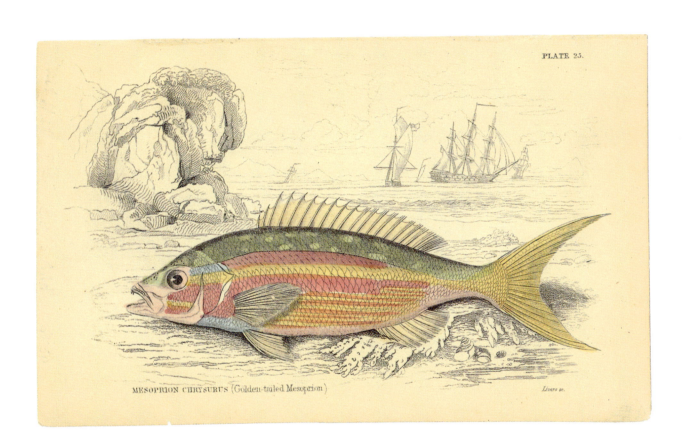

PLATE 25.

MESOPRION CHRYSURUS (Golden-tailed Mesoprion)

Lizars sc.

Each fish, which every channell hath,

Will amorously to thee swimme,

Gladder to catch thee, then thou him.

If thou, to be so seene, beest loath,

By Sunne, or Moone, thou darknest both,

And if my selfe have leave to see,

I need not their light, having thee.

Let others freeze with angling reeds,

And cut their legges, with shells and weeds,

Or treacherously poore fish beset,

With strangling snare, or windowie net:

Let coarse bold hands, from slimy nest

The bedded fish in banks out-wrest,

Or curious traitors, sleavesilke flies

Bewitch poore fishes wandring eyes.

For thee, thou needst no such deceit,

For thou thy selfe art thine owne baite;

That fish, that is not catch'd thereby,

Alas, is wiser farre than I.

PLATE XI.

SUDIS GIGAS.

ROBERT PENN WARREN

The Red Mullet

THE FIG FLAMES inward on the bough, and I,

Deep where the great mullet, red, lounges in

Black shadow of the shoal, have come. Where no light may

Come, he, the great one, like flame, burns, and I

Have met him, eye to eye, the lower jaw horn,

Outthrust, arched down at the corners, merciless as

Genghis, motionless and mogul, and the eye of

The mullet is round, bulging, ringed like a target

In gold, vision is armor, he sees and does not

Stewart delt.

1 *The Smelt or Sparling*

PLATE 1.

Lizars sc.

Grayling

Forgive. The mullet has looked me in the eye, and forgiven

Nothing. At night I fear suffocation, is there

Enough air in the world for us all, therefore I

Swim much, dive deep to develop my lung-case, I am

Familiar with the agony of will in the deep place. Blood

Thickens as oxygen fails. Oh, mullet, thy flame

Burns in the shadow of the black shoal.

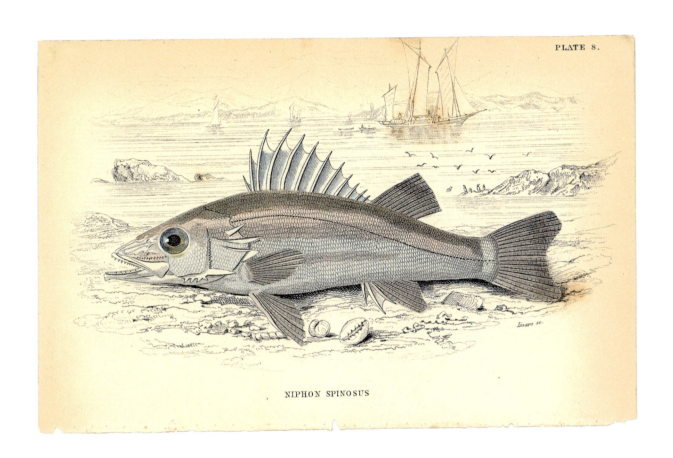

PLATE 8.

NIPHON SPINOSUS

PLATE 19.

Gymnotus fasciatus

Stewart del.t   Lizars sc.

Herman Melville

Squid

SLOWLY WADING THROUGH the meadows of brit, the
Pequod still held on her way north-eastward towards the island of
Java; a gentle air impelling her keel, so that in the surrounding
serenity her three tall tapering masts mildly waved to that languid
breeze, as three mild palms on a plain. And still, at wide intervals in
the silvery night, the lonely, alluring jet would be seen.

But one transparent blue morning, when a stillness almost
preternatural spread over the sea, however unattended with any
stagnant calm; when the long burnished sun-glade on the waters
seemed a golden finger laid across them, enjoining some secresy;
when the slippered waves whispered together as they softly ran on;

in this profound hush of the visible sphere a strange spectre was seen by Daggoo from the main-mast head.

In the distance, a great white mass lazily rose, and rising higher and higher, and disentangling itself from the azure, at last gleamed before our prow like a snow-slide, new slid from the hills. Thus glistening for a moment, as slowly it subsided, and sank. Then once more arose, and silently gleamed. It seemed not a whale; and yet is this Moby Dick? thought Daggoo. Again the phantom went down, but on reappearing once more, with a stiletto-like cry that startled every man from his nod, the negro yelled out— "There! there again! there she breaches! right ahead! The White Whale, the White Whale!"

Upon this, the seamen rushed to the yard-arms, as in swarming-time the bees rush to the boughs. Bare-headed in the sultry sun, Ahab stood on the bowsprit, and with one hand pushed far behind in readiness to wave his orders to the helmsman, cast his eager glance in the direction indicated aloft by the outstretched motionless arm of Daggoo.

Whether the flitting attendance of the one still and solitary

PLATE 21.

European Pile fish.

Stewart del.

Belo

PLATE 1.

ianensis.

Lizars sc.

jet had gradually worked upon Ahab, so that he was now prepared to connect the ideas of mildness and repose with the first sight of the particular whale he pursued; however this was, or whether his eagerness betrayed him; whichever way it might have been, no sooner did he distinctly perceive the white mass, than with a quick intensity he instantly gave orders for lowering.

The four boats were soon on the water; Ahab's in advance, and all swiftly pulling towards their prey. Soon it went down, and while, with oars suspended, we were awaiting its reappearance, lo! in the same spot where it sank, once more it slowly rose. Almost forgetting for the moment all thoughts of Moby Dick, we now gazed at the wondrous phenomenon which the secret seas have hitherto revealed to mankind. A vast pulpy mass, furlongs in length and breadth, of a glancing cream-color, lay floating on the water, innumerable long arms radiating from its centre, and curling and twisting like a nest of anacondas, as if blindly to clutch at any hapless object within reach. No perceptible face or front did it have; no conceivable token of either sensation or instinct; but undulated there on the billows, an unearthly, formless, chance-like apparition of life.

As with a low sucking sound it slowly disappeared again, Starbuck still gazing at the agitated waters where it had sunk, with a wild voice exclaimed—"Almost rather had I seen Moby Dick and fought him, than to have seen thee, thou white ghost!"

"What was it, Sir?" said Flask.

"The great live squid, which, they say, few whale-ships ever beheld, and returned to their ports to tell of it."

But Ahab said nothing; turning his boat, he sailed back to the vessel; the rest as silently following.

Whatever superstitions the sperm whalemen in general have connected with the sight of this object, certain it is, that a glimpse of it being so very unusual, that circumstance has gone far to invest it with portentousness. So rarely is it beheld, that though one and all of them declare it to be the largest animated thing in the ocean, yet very few of them have any but the most vague ideas concerning its true nature and form; notwithstanding, they believe it to furnish to the sperm whale his only food. For though other species of whales find their food above water, and may be seen by man in the act of feeding, the spermaceti whale obtains his whole

PLATE 22.

FOUR-HORNED ASPIDOPHORUS.

Lizars sc

food in unknown zones below the surface; and only by inference
is it that any one can tell of what, precisely, that food consists.
At times, when closely pursued, he will disgorge what are supposed
to be the detached arms of the squid; some of them thus exhibited
exceeding twenty and thirty feet in length. They fancy that the
monster to which these arms belonged ordinarily clings by them to
the bed of the ocean; and that the sperm whale, unlike other species,
is supplied with teeth in order to attack and tear it.

There seems some ground to imagine that the great Kraken
of Bishop Pontoppodan may ultimately resolve itself into Squid.
The manner in which the Bishop describes it, as alternately rising
and sinking, with some other particulars he narrates, in all this the
two correspond. But much abatement is necessary with respect to
the incredible bulk he assigns it.

By some naturalists who have vaguely heard rumors of the
mysterious creature, here spoken of, it is included among the class
of cuttlefish, to which, indeed, in certain external respects it would
seem to belong, but only as the Anak of the tribe.

NICK LYONS

The Metamorphosis

MY FRIEND CLYDE awoke one morning from uneasy dreams to find himself transformed in the night into a gigantic brown trout. It was no joke. He looked around him, hoping to see his pleasant little one-room apartment where he had lived a hermetic life since his wife cashiered him. Its walls were papered with color photographs of rising trout and natural flies the size of grouse; each corner held three or four bamboo rods in aluminum tubes; the chests of drawers were crammed with blue-dun necks and flies and fly boxes and his thirteen Princess reels; the windowsills and bookcases were packed solid with hundreds of books and catalogs and magazines devoted to the sport to which he had devoted his life. They were not there.

PLATE 18

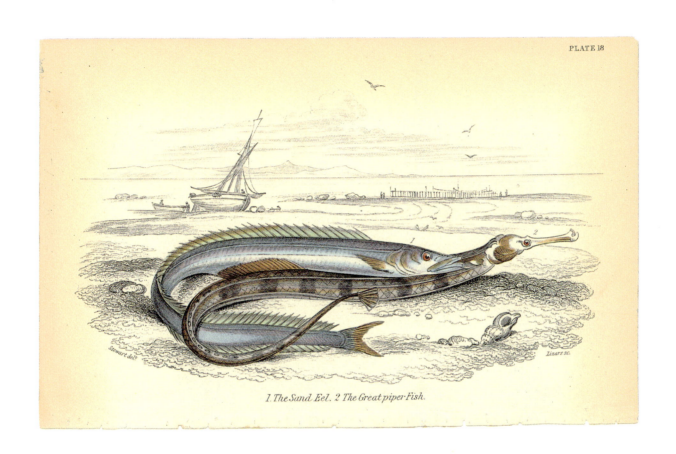

1. The Sand Eel. 2 The Great piper Fish.

Neither were his hands, which were fins.

Instead, he was suspended in cold moving water under an old upturned maple stump. From the clarity and size of the water, he deduced he was in Montana, or perhaps Idaho. That was fine with Clyde. If he was going to be a trout, and he had often meditated on what it would be like to be a trout (so he could tell how they thought), he'd just as well be one in Montana and Idaho.

"Well, this love of fly fishing sure takes me places I otherwise wouldn't go," he thought.

And as soon as he thought this, he realized, since he was thinking, that he had resolved an age-old problem. If he, existing under that old tree stump, could think, he could analyze his own thoughts; and since what was true for him would have to be true for all trout, he could learn what any trout thought. He was glad he had read Descartes and Kant before he went on the Halford binge.

Curiously, his esoteric studies had led him closer and closer to this point. Only the night before he had been sitting in the dimly lit room, sunk deep into his armchair in front of the lit fish-tank in which swam Oscar, his pet brown. He had been staring intently, reciting a mantra, meditating, as he did every night for four hours, when, for a moment—no, it could not be true—Oscar had (at least he thought so) told him that Foolex dubbing was the ultimate solution to the body problem. "Not quill ribbing?" he had asked audibly. "Definitely not," said Oscar. "I like you so I'll give you the straight poop: Foolex is where it's at. Anyway, tomorrow it . . . oh, you'll find out."

And so he had.

He had a thousand questions and worked his way a bit upstream, where he saw a pretty spotted tail waving gently back and forth. The trout, a hen, about three pounds, shifted slightly as Clyde nudged her and eyed him suspiciously: it was still three weeks before spawning season and she was feeling none too frisky. He opened his mouth to ask her about Foolex bodies and careened back in the current. The henfish, named Trudy, thought he was a dumb cluck and that she ought to work her way quickly past the riffle into the upper pool. Maybe this bird's clock was wrong; though she had a rotten headache, he might even attack her.

Clyde, ever watchful, immediately deduced from her defensiveness that communication among trout, like communication

PLATE 15.

ASPRO VULGARIS
(View on the Rhone)

Lizars sc.

between fly fishermen and bocce players, was impossible. He'd have to answer his questions by himself. This is never easy, particularly not on an empty stomach. He had not eaten anything since the pepperoni sandwich fifteen hours earlier; and he was not dumb enough to think he could soon get another, since the Belle Deli was two thousand miles away.

There was a silver flash and Clyde turned and shot up after it, turning on it as it slowed and turned and lifted up in the current. But he was too late. A little twelve-inch rainbow had sped from behind a large rock and grasped the thing, and it was now struggling with ludicrous futility across stream, the silver object stuck in its lower jaw.

"Incredible!" Clyde thought. "How could I have been so dumb?" He had not seen the hooks; he had not distinguished between metal and true scales. If he who had studied Halford, Skues, Marinaro, and Schwiebert could not distinguish a C.P. Swing from a dace tartare, what hope had any of his speckled kin? He shivered with fear as he asked himself: "Are *all* trout this dumb?"

He worked his way back under the upturned stump, into the

eddy, and sulked. This was a grim business. He noticed he was trembling with acute anxiety neurosis but could not yet accept that *all* trout were neurotic. He was positively starved now and would have risen to spinach, which he hated.

Bits and pieces of debris, empty nymph shucks, a couple of grubs swept into the eddy. He nosed them, bumped them, took them into his mouth, spit some of them out. By noon he had managed to nudge loose one half-dead stone-fly nymph, *Pteronarcys californica*; he had nabbed one measly earthworm; and he had found a few cased caddises. Most food, he noted, came off the bottom; that's where it was at. The lure had come down from the surface; he should have known. He was learning something new every minute.

By now he had recognized that he was in the Big Hole River, below Divide; he was sure he had once fished the pool. Settled into that eddy under the stump, he now knew why he had not raised a fish here: the current swung the food down below the undercut bank, but his flies had been too high up in the water. The way to fish this run was almost directly downstream from his present position, casting parallel to the bank so the nymph would have a chance to ride low and slip down into the eddy.

He was trying to plot the physics of the thing, from below, and was getting dizzy, when he realized he could starve flat down to death if he didn't stop trying to be a trout fisherman and settle for being a trout. His stomach felt pinched and dry; his jaws ached to clamp down on a fresh stone-fly nymph or, yes, a grasshopper. That's what he wanted. He suddenly had a mad letch for grasshoppers—and there was absolutely nothing he could do to get one. He was totally dependent upon chance. "A trout's lot," he thought, "is not a happy one."

Just then the surface rippled a bit, perhaps from a breeze, and a couple of yards upstream, he saw the telltale yellow body, kicking legs, and molded head of a grasshopper. It was August, and he knew the grasshoppers grew large around the Big Hole at that time of the year. It came at him quickly, he rose sharply to it, then stopped and turned away with a smirk. "Not me. Uh-uh. A Dave's Hopper if I ever saw one. Not for this guy." And as he thought this, Trudy swept downstream past him, too quick for him to warn, and nabbed the thing in an abrupt little splash. Then she turned, swam up by him, seemed to shake her head and say, "How dumb a cluck can you be?"

Stewart delt

Native of

PLATE 21.

S PACU.

sequibo, Guiana.

Lizars sc.

So it *had* been the real thing. Nature was imitating art now. Oh, he could taste the succulent hopper.

Another splatted down, juicy and alive, and he rose again, paused, and it shot downstream in a rush. He'd never know about that one.

Oh, the existential torment of it! "And I thought deciding which artificial fly to use was hard!"

Two more hoppers, then a third splatted down. He passed up one, lost a fin-race with Trudy for the third. She was becoming a pill.

He could bear it no longer. He'd even eat a Nick's Crazylegs if it came down. Anything. Anything to be done with the torment, the veil of unknowing, the inscrutability, which was worse than the pain in his gut, as it always is.

And then he saw it.

It was a huge, preposterous, feathered thing with a big black hook curled up under it. Some joker with three thumbs had thought it looked like a grasshopper. The body was made of Foolex. How could Oscar possibly have thought that body anything other than insulting? Clyde's hook jaw turned up in a wry smile; he wiggled his adipose fin. The fly came down over him and he watched it safely from his eddy. And it came down again. Then again. Twelve. Thirteen times. Trudy had moved twice in its direction. He could tell she was getting fairly neurotic about it.

Foolex? That body could not fool an imbecile. It *was* an insult!

Eighteen. Twenty times the monstrosity came over him. He was fuming now. How dare someone throw something like that at him! Had they no respect whatsoever? If that's all fishermen thought of him, what did it matter. He was bored and hungry and suffering from a severe case of *angst* and humiliation. Nothing mattered. It was a trout's life.

He rose quickly and surely now, turning as the thing swept down past him on the thirty-third cast. He saw it hang in \the surface eddy for a moment. He opened his mouth. Foolex? It infuriated him! It was the ultimate insult.

He lunged forward. And at the precise moment he knew exactly what trout see and why they strike, he stopped being a trout.

PLATE 16

The Murana.

HANS CHRISTIAN ANDERSEN

The Great Sea Serpent

THERE ONCE WAS a little fish. He was of good family; his name
I have forgotten—if you want to know it, you must ask someone
learned in these matters. He had one thousand and eight hundred
brothers and sisters, all born at the same time. They did not know
their parents and had to take care of themselves. They swam around
happily in the sea. They had enough water to drink—all the great
oceans of the world. They did not speculate upon where their food
would come from, that would come by itself. Each wanted to follow
his own inclinations and live his own life; not that they gave much
thought to that either.

The sun shone down into the sea and illuminated the water.

It was a strange world, filled with the most fantastic creatures; some of them were so big and had such huge jaws that they could have swallowed all eighteen hundred of the little fish at once. But this, too, they did not worry about, for none of them had been eaten yet.

The little fishes swam close together, as herring or mackerel do. They were thinking about nothing except swimming. Suddenly they heard a terrible noise, and from the surface of the sea a great thing was cast among them. There was more and more of it; it was endless and had neither head nor tail. It was heavy and every one of the small fishes that it hit was either stunned and thrown aside or had its back broken.

The fishes—big and small, the ones who lived up near the waves and those who dwelled in the depths—all fled, while this monstrous serpent grew longer and longer as it sank deeper and deeper, until at last it was hundreds of miles long, and lay at the bottom of the sea, crossing the whole ocean.

All the fishes—yes, even the snails and all the other animals that live in the sea—saw or heard about the strange, gigantic, unknown eel that had descended into the sea from the air above.

What was it? We know that it was the telegraph cable, thousands of miles long, that human beings had laid to connect America and Europe.

All the inhabitants of the sea were frightened of this new huge animal that had come to live among them. The flying fishes leaped up from the sea and into the air; and the gurnard since it knew how, shot up out of the water like a bullet. Others went down into the depths of the ocean so fast that they were there before the telegraph cable. They frightened both the cod and the flounder, who were swimming around peacefully, hunting and eating their fellow creatures.

A couple of sea cucumbers were so petrified that they spat out their own stomachs in fright; but they survived, for they knew how to swallow them again. Lots of lobsters and crabs left their shells in the confusion. During all this, the eighteen hundred little fishes were separated; most of them never saw one another again, nor would they have recognized one another if they had. Only a dozen of them stayed in the same spot, and after they had lain still a couple of hours their worst fright was over and curiosity became stronger than fear.

They looked about, both above and below themselves, and there at the bottom of the sea they thought they saw the monster that had frightened them all. It looked thin, but who knew how big it could make itself or how strong it was. It lay very still, but it might be up to something.

The more timid of the small fish said, "Let it lie where it is, it is no concern of ours." But the tiniest of them were determined to find out what it was. Since the monster had come from above, it was better to seek information about it up there. They swam up to the surface of the ocean. The wind was still and the sea was like a mirror.

They met a dolphin. He is a fellow who likes to jump and to turn somersaults in the sea. The dolphin has eyes to see with and ought to have seen what happened, and therefore the little fishes approached it. But a dolphin only thinks about himself and his somersaults; he didn't know what to say, so he didn't say anything, but looked very proud.

A seal came swimming by just at that moment, and even though it eats small fishes, it was more polite than the dolphin.

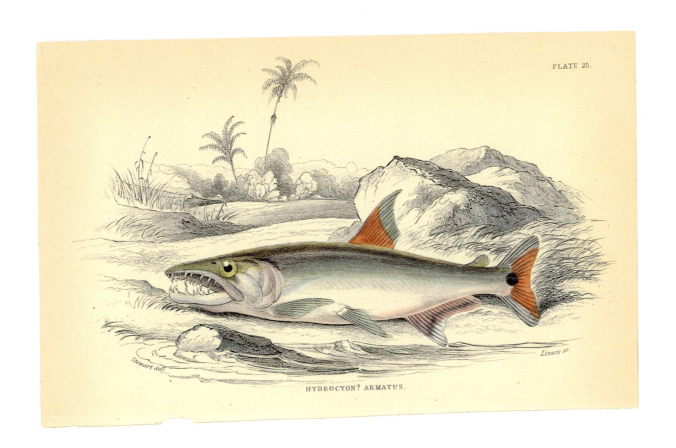

PLATE 25.

Stewart del.

Lizars sc.

HYDROCYON? ARMATUS.

Luckily it happened to be full, and it knew more than the jumping fish. "Many a night have I lain on a wet stone—miles and miles away from here—and looked toward land, where live those treacherous creatures who call themselves, in their own language, men. They are always hunting me and my kind, though usually we manage to escape. That is exactly what happened to the great sea serpent that you are asking about—it got away from them. They had had it in their power for ever so long, and kept it up on land. Now men wanted to transport it to another country, across the sea.—Why? you may ask, but I can't answer.—They had a lot of trouble getting it on board the ship. But they finally succeeded; after all, it was weakened from its stay on land. They rolled it up, round and round into a coil. It wiggled and writhed, and what a lot of noise it made! I heard it. When the ship got out to sea, the great eel slipped overboard. They tried to stop it. I saw them, there were dozens of hands holding onto its body. But they couldn't. Now it is lying down at the bottom of the sea, and I guess it will stay there for a while."

"It looks awfully thin," said the tiny fishes.

"They have starved it," explained the seal. "But it will soon get its old figure and strength back. I am sure it is the great sea serpent: the one men are so afraid of that they talk about it all the time. I had not believed it existed, but now I do. And that was it." With a flip of its tail, the seal dived and was gone.

"How much he knew and how well he talked," said one of the little fishes admiringly. "I have never known so much as I do now—I just hope it wasn't all lies."

"We could swim down and look," suggested the tiniest of the tiny fishes. "And on the way down we could hear what the other fishes think."

"We wouldn't move a fin to know anything more," said all the other tiny fishes, turned, and swam away.

"But I will," shouted the tiniest one, and swam down into the depths. But he was far away from where the great sea serpent had sunk. The little fish searched in every direction. Never had he realized that the world was so big. Great shoals of herring glided by like silver boats, and behind them came schools of mackerel that were even more splendid and brilliant. There were fishes of all shapes, with all kinds of markings and colors. Jellyfish, looking like

PLATE 1.

OPHISURUS.

Lizars sc.

transparent plants, floated by, carried by the currents. Down at
the bottom of the sea the strangest things grew: tall grasses and
palm-shaped trees whose every leaf was covered with crustaceans.

At last the tiny fish spied a long dark line far below it and
swam down to it. It was not the giant serpent but the railing of a
sunken ship, whose upper and lower decks had been torn in two by
the pressure of the sea. The little fish entered the great cabin, where
the terrified passengers had gathered as the ship went down; they
had all drowned and the currents of the sea had carried their bodies
away, except for two of them: a young woman who lay on a bench
with her babe in her arms. The sea rocked them gently; they looked
as though they were sleeping. The little fish grew frightened as he
looked at them. What if they were to wake? The cabin was so quiet
and so lonely that the tiny fish hurried away again, out into the
light, where there were other fishes. It had not swum very far when
it met a young whale; it was awfully big.

"Please don't swallow me," pleaded the little fish. "I am
so little you could hardly taste me, and I find it such a great pleasure
to live."

"What are you doing down here?" grunted the whale. "It is much too deep for your kind." Then the tiny fish told the whale about the greet eel—or whatever it could be—that had come from the air and descended into the sea, frightening even the most courageous fishes.

"Ha, ha, ha!" laughed the whale, and swallowed so much water that it had to surface in order to breathe and spout the water out. "Ho-ho . . . ha-ha. That must have been the thing that tickled my back when I was turning over. I thought it was the mast of a ship and was just about to use it as a back scratcher; but it must have been that. It lies farther out. I think I will go and have a look at it; I haven't anything else to do."

The whale swam away and the tiny fish followed it, but not too closely for the great animal left a turbulent wake behind it.

They met a shark and an old sawfish. They, too, had heard about the strange great eel that was so thin and yet longer than any other fish. They hadn't seen it but wanted to.

A catfish joined them. "If that sea serpent is not thicker than an anchor cable, then I will cut it in two, in one bite," he said, and

opened his monstrous jaws to show his six rows of teeth. "If I can
make a mark in an anchor I guess I can bite a stem like that in two."

"There it is," cried the whale. "Look how it moves,
twisting and turning." The whale thought he had better eyesight
than the others. As a matter of fact he hadn't; what he had seen was
merely an old conger eel, several yards long, that was swimming
toward them.

"That fellow has never caused any commotion in the sea
before, or frightened any other big fish," said the catfish with
disgust. "I have met him often."

They told the conger about the new sea serpent and asked
him if he wanted to go with them to discover what it was.

"I wonder if it is longer than I am," said the conger eel, and
stretched himself. "If it is, then it will be sorry."

"It certainly will," said the rest of the company. "There are
enough of us so we don't have to tolerate it if we don't want to!"
they exclaimed, and hurried on.

They saw something that looked like a floating island
that was having trouble keeping itself from sinking. It was an old

PLATE 13

1 Black Fish. 2. Pilas Fish.

whale. His head was overgrown with seaweed, and on his back were so many mussels and oysters that its black skin looked as if it had white spots.

"Come on, old man," the young whale said. "There is a new fish in the ocean and we won't tolerate it!"

"Oh, let me stay where I am!" grumbled the old whale. "Peace is all I ask, to be left in peace. Ow! Ow! . . . I am very sick, it will be the death of me. My only comfort is to let my back emerge above the water, then the sea gulls scratch it: the sweet birds. That helps a lot as long as they don't dig too deep with their bills and get into the blubber. There's the skeleton of one still sitting on my back. It got stuck and couldn't get loose when I had to submerge. The little fishes picked his bones clean. You can see it. . . . Look at him, and look at me. . . . Oh, I am very sick."

"You are just imagining all that," said the young whale. "I am not sick, no one that lives in the sea is ever sick."

"I am sorry!" said the old whale. "The eels have skin diseases, the carp have smallpox, and we all suffer from worms."

"Nonsense!" shouted the shark, who didn't like to listen to

that kind of talk. Neither did the others, so they all swam on.

At last they came to the place where part of the telegraph cable lies, that stretches from Europe to America across sand shoals and high mountains, through endless forests of seaweed and coral. The currents move as the winds do in the heavens above, and through them swim schools of fishes, more numerous than the flocks of migratory birds that fly through the air. There was a noise, a sound, a humming, the ghost of which you hear in the great conch shell when you hold it up to your ear.

"There is the serpent!" shouted the bigger fish and the little fishes too. They had caught sight of some of the telegraph cable but neither the beginning nor the end of it, for they were both lost in the far distance. Sponges, polyps, and gorgonia swayed above it and leaned against it, sometimes hiding it from view. Sea urchins and snails climbed over it; and great crabs, like giant spiders, walked tightrope along it. Deep blue sea cucumbers—or whatever those creatures are called who eat with their whole body—lay next to it; one would think that they were trying to smell it. Flounders and cod kept turning from side to side, in order to be able to listen to

Sussex del.   Lizars sc
1. THE SEA BREAM.   2. THE AXILLARY

what everyone was saying. The starfishes had dug themselves down in the mire; only two of their points were sticking up, but they had eyes on them and were staring at the black snake, hoping to see something come out of it.

The telegraph cable lay perfectly still, as if it were lifeless; but inside, it was filled with life: with thoughts, human thoughts.

"That thing is treacherous," said the whale. "It might hit me in the stomach, and that is my weak point."

"Let's feel our way forward," said one of the polyps. "I have long arms and flexible fingers. I've already touched it, but now I'll take a firmer grasp."

And it stuck out its arms and encircled the cable. "I have felt both its stomach and its back. It is not scaly. I don't think it has any skin either. I don't believe it lays eggs and I don't think it gives birth to live children."

The conger eel lay down beside the cable and stretched itself as far as it could. "It is longer than I am," it admitted. "But length isn't everything. One has to have skin, a good stomach and, above all, suppleness."

The whale—the young strong whale!—bowed more deeply than it ever had before. "Are you a fish or a plant?" he asked. "Or are you a surface creation, one of those who can't live down here?"

The telegraph didn't answer, though it was filled with words. Thoughts traveled through it so fast that they took only seconds to move from one end to the other: hundreds of miles away.

"Will you answer or be bitten in two?" asked the ill-mannered shark.

All the other fishes repeated the question: "Answer or be bitten in two?"

The telegraph cable didn't move; it had its own ideas, which isn't surprising for someone so full of thoughts. "Let them bite me in two," it thought. "Then I will be pulled up and repaired. It has happened to lots of my relations, that are not half as long as I am." But it didn't speak, it telegraphed; besides, it found the question impertinent; after all, it was lying there on official business.

Dusk had come. The sun was setting, as men say. It was fiery red, and the clouds were as brilliant as fire—one more beautiful than the other.

"Now comes the red illumination," said the polyp. "Maybe the thing will be easier to see in that light, though I hardly think it worth looking at."

"Attack it! Attack it!" screamed the catfish, and showed all his teeth.

"Attack it! Attack it!" shouted the whale, the shark, the swordfish, and the conger eel.

They pushed forward. The catfish was first; but just as it was going to bite the cable the swordfish, who was a little too eager, stuck its sword into the behind of the catfish. It was a mistake, but it kept the catfish from using the full strength of its jaw muscles.

There was a great muddle in the mud. The sea cucumbers, the big fishes, and the small ones swam around in circles; they pushed and shoved and squashed and ate each other up. The crabs and the lobsters fought, and the snails pulled their heads into their houses. The telegraph cable just minded its own business, which is the proper thing for a telegraph cable to do.

Night came to the sky above, but down in the ocean millions and millions of little animals illuminated the water. Crayfish no

larger than the head of a pin gave off light. It is incredible and
wonderful; and quite true.

All the animals of the sea looked at the telegraph cable.
"If only we knew what it was—or at least what it wasn't," said one
of the fishes. And that was a very important question.

An old sea cow—human beings call them mermen and
mermaids—came gliding by. This one was a mermaid. She had a tail
and short arms for splashing, hanging breasts, and seaweed and
parasites on her head—and of these she was very proud. "If you
want learning and knowledge," she said, "then I think I am the best
equipped to give it to you. But I want free passage on the bottom of
the sea for myself and my family. I am a fish like you, and a reptile by
training. I am the most intelligent citizen of the ocean. I know about
everything under the water and everything above it. The thing that
you are worrying about comes from up there; and everything from
above is dead and powerless, once it comes down here. So let it lie,
it is only a human invention and of no importance."

"I think it may be more than that," said the tiny fish.

"Shut up, mackerel!" said the sea cow.

PLATE 19

Wolf Fish.

"Shrimp!" shouted the others, and they meant it as an insult.

The sea cow explained to them that the sea serpent who had frightened them—the cable itself, by the way, didn't make a sound—was not dangerous. It was only an invention of those animals up on dry land called human beings. When she finished talking about the sea serpent, she gave a little lesson in the craftiness and wickedness of men: "They are always trying to catch us. That is the only reason for their existence. They throw down nets, traps, and long fishing lines that have hooks, with bait attached to them, to try and fool us. This is probably another—bigger—fishing line. They are so stupid that they expect us to bite on it. But we aren't as dumb as that. Don't touch that piece of junk. It will unravel, fall apart, and become mud and mire—the whole thing. Let it lie there and rot. Anything that comes from above is worthless; it breaks or creaks; it is no good!"

"No good!" said all the creatures of the sea, accepting the mermaid's opinion in order to have one.

The little tiny fish didn't agree, but it had learned to keep its thoughts to itself. "That enormously long snake may be the most marvelous fish in the sea. I have a feeling that it is."

"Marvelous!" we human beings agree; and we can prove that it is true.

The great sea serpent of the fable has become a fact. It was constructed by human skill, conceived by human intelligence. It stretches from the Eastern Hemisphere to the Western, carrying messages from country to country faster than light travels from the sun down to the earth. Each year the great serpent grows. Soon it will stretch across all the great oceans, under the storm-whipped waves and the glasslike water, through which the skipper can look down as if he were sailing through the air and see the multitude of fish and the fireworks of color.

At the very depths is a *Midgards-worm*, biting its own tail as it circumscribes the world. Fish and reptiles hit their heads against it: it is impossible to understand what it is by looking at it. Human thoughts expressed in all the languages of the world, and yet silent: the snake of knowledge of good and evil. The most wonderful of the wonders of the sea: our time's great sea serpent!

PLATE 13.

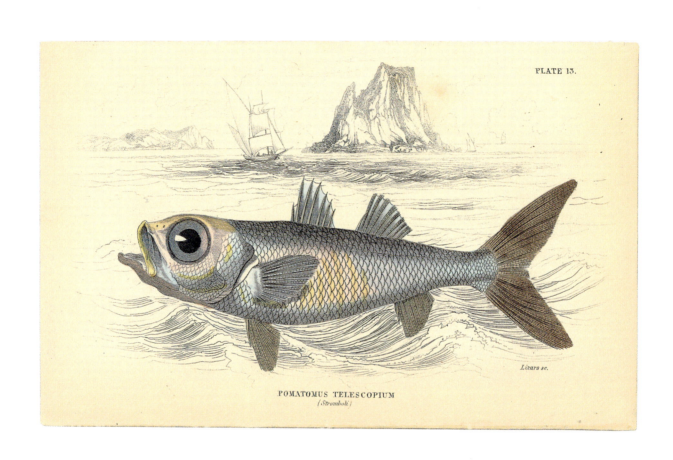

POMATOMUS TELESCOPIUM
(Stromboli)

Lizars sc.

EDUARDO GALEANO

Rain

IN CHILE HE has seen a lot of dying, his dearest friends shot, beaten, or kicked to death. Juan Bustos, one of President Allende's advisers, has saved himself by a hair.

Exiled in Honduras, Juan drags out his days. Of those who died in Chile, how many died instead of him? From whom is he stealing the air he breathes? He has been this way for months, dragging himself from sorrow to sorrow, ashamed of surviving, when one evening his feet take him to a town called Yoro, in the central depths of Honduras.

He arrives in Yoro for no particular reason, and in Yoro spends the night under any old roof. He gets up very early and starts walking half-heartedly through the dirt streets, fearing melancholy, staring without seeing.

Suddenly, the rain hits him, so violent that Juan covers his head, though noticing right away that this prodigious rain isn't water or hail. Crazy silver lights bounce off the ground and jump through the air.

"*It's raining fish!*" cries Juan, slapping at the live fish that dive down from the clouds and leap and sparkle around him. Never again will it occur to him to curse the miracle of being alive, never again will he forget that he had the luck to be born in America.

"*That's right,*" says a neighbor, quietly, as if it were nothing. "*Here in Yoro it rains fish.*"

PLATE 15.

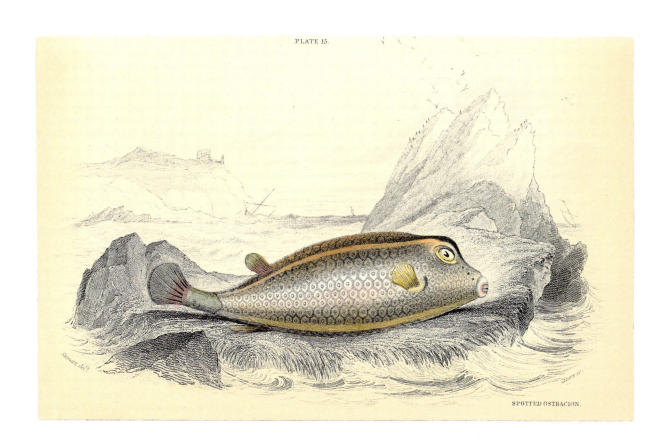

SPOTTED OSTRACION.

Lizars drawings courtesy of
Lyons Ltd., San Francisco

Special thanks to Tom Morgan,
Judith Schnell, and David Detweiler.

JOHN MILLER runs Big Fish, a book packaging company in
San Francisco. Big Fish has produced a number of art books and literary
anthologies, most recently *Noa Noa: Paul Gauguin's Notebooks*, and a
fine art edition, *Marlin!* by Ernest Hemingway. He has also been an art
director at *Vanity Fair*, *Esquire*, and *Panorama* in Milan.

PERMISSIONS ACKNOWLEDGMENTS

"Shining Fish" from *Italian Folktales: Selected and Retold* by Italo Calvino, translated
by George Martin, ©1956 by Giulio Einaudi editore, s.p.a., English ©1980 by
Harcourt Brace Jovanovich, Inc.

"The Fish" from *The Complete Poems 1927-1979* by Elizabeth Bishop. ©1979, 1983
by Alice Helen Methfessel. Reprinted by permission of Farrar, Straus & Giroux.

"The Big Fish" by Blake LeLand ©1991 by Blake LeLand. Reprinted by permission
of *The New Yorker* Magazine.

"Dante and the Lobster" from *More Pricks Than Kicks* by Samuel Beckett, ©1972
by Grove Press, Inc. Used with the permission of Grove Press, Inc.

"The Red Mullet" from *Incarnations: Poems 1966-1968*, by Robert Penn Warren.
©1968 by Robert Penn Warren. Reprinted by permission of Random House, Inc.

"The Metamorphosis" from *Confessions of a Fly Fishing Addict*, by Nick Lyons ©1989 by
Nick Lyons. Reprinted by permission Fireside Books, a division of Simon & Schuster.

"Rain" from *Memory of Fire, Volume III: Century of the Wind* by Eduardo Galeano
©1988 by Cedric Belfrage. Reprinted by permission of Pantheon Books,
a division of Random House, Inc.

Pl. 58.

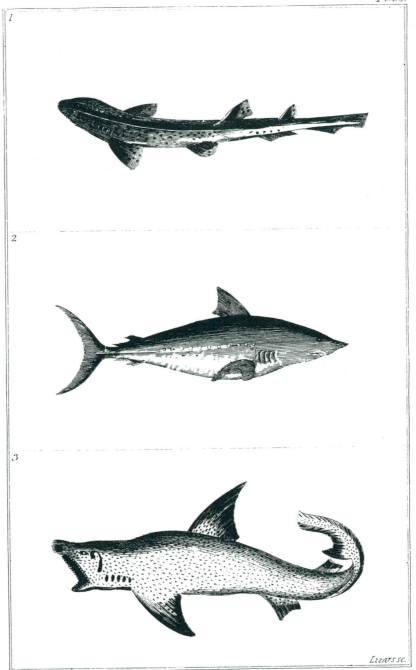

1. *Lesser Spotted Shark* 2. *Porbeagle D.º* 3. *White D.º*